CW01238433

Holding Grace

Prose & Poetry

Best Wishes!

RJ HELLER

Balboa Press
A DIVISION OF HAY HOUSE

Copyright © 2013 RJ Heller.

All rights reserved. No part of this book may be used or reproduced by any means, graphic, electronic, or mechanical, including photocopying, recording, taping or by any information storage retrieval system without the written permission of the publisher except in the case of brief quotations embodied in critical articles and reviews.

Balboa Press books may be ordered through booksellers or by contacting:

*Balboa Press
A Division of Hay House
1663 Liberty Drive
Bloomington, IN 47403
www.balboapress.com
1-(877) 407-4847*

Because of the dynamic nature of the Internet, any web addresses or links contained in this book may have changed since publication and may no longer be valid. The views expressed in this work are solely those of the author and do not necessarily reflect the views of the publisher, and the publisher hereby disclaims any responsibility for them.

The author of this book does not dispense medical advice or prescribe the use of any technique as a form of treatment for physical, emotional, or medical problems without the advice of a physician, either directly or indirectly. The intent of the author is only to offer information of a general nature to help you in your quest for emotional and spiritual well-being. In the event you use any of the information in this book for yourself, which is your constitutional right, the author and the publisher assume no responsibility for your actions.

*Any people depicted in stock imagery provided by Thinkstock are models, and such images are being used for illustrative purposes only.
Certain stock imagery © Thinkstock.*

*Black & White Photos by RJ Heller
Cover Photo by Shaun Bell, Johannesburg, South Africa
Back Cover Photo by Caitlin Heller, Nashville, TN*

*ISBN: 978-1-4525-7712-8 (sc)
ISBN: 978-1-4525-7711-1 (e)*

Library of Congress Control Number: 2013911482

Printed in the United States of America.

Balboa Press rev. date: 09/13/2013

Grace | gras |

do honor or credit to (someone or something)
by one's presence

Oxford American Dictionary

*In everything that is,
there is something that was.*

To family and friends—your thoughts,
wishes, and support made this happen. I am graced
by your presence and am ever thankful for you
being in my life.

To that editor both outside and in—the smiles continue,
as I do not know where they (the words) come from.
Thank you!

Preface

With *Holding Grace* I am simply trying to tell a story of those lifetime moments we all have had, and wish we could have again. The pieces are simple and reflective while being purposeful and completely accessible, which is just how life should be lived. They are personal and, at the same time, universal, as I believe we all touch and share our lives with one another in some way, shape, or form, making us one as we move forward in life and take that next step.

In closing, I will let the words of two dear friends tell of their experience with *Holding Grace*, and hope that you will find a memory or two from your own life, hidden amongst the words within these pages. Enjoy!

I'm a musician, so the thing that grabs me the most about Rick's work is his way of describing things in a musical way. I think if he composed music, it would be very much like my own: full of reflection and nostalgia. This collection echoes my own feelings through words, whereas I only have the creative capacity to translate these emotions into music. I especially enjoyed "An Evening of Grace." Life is all about pausing to enjoy the little things and reflecting on moments that we can never get back. It's a delicate balance of holding on and letting go; carefully soaking in the rain and letting it wash over us while not washing us away.

Josh Kramer
Composer
Tarsus, Turkey

The first time I read Rick's writing, the power and depth of his words swept me off my feet. He has a unique ability to make something wonderful of everyday things. There is so much warmth and feeling in his words that one simply cannot put it down before you have read and enjoyed every bit of it. "A Morning Made of Perfection" is a personal favorite.

Elizabeth Kendall
Artist
Bronkhorstspruit, Gauteng, South Africa

Contents

BOOK ONE
Bits

A Man and Tree 3
Clouds 4
Mountains 5
Stones 7
Streams 8
Trees 9
Of Trees Singing 10
Shade to Time 11
Safe Harbor 13
Rows of Corn 14

BOOK TWO
Some Pieces

Steps Taken 19
As I Wait 23
Night Sky 24
Between the Tides 25
Home 27
Beginnings 28

~ xiii ~

The Sound of Rain 30
An Endless Pause 32
The Touch of Another 34
Ebb Tide 37

BOOK THREE

And Story

An Evening of Grace 41
As Water Beckons 43
A Journey 46
Touching of Souls 47
Possession Morning 50
Holding Grace 53
Washed Anew 57
Beyond Beautiful 63
A Morning Made of Perfection 67

BOOK ONE

Bits

A Man and Tree

Nature in Five-Part Harmony:

Clouds

Mountains

Stones

Streams

Trees

Of Trees Singing

Shade to Time

Safe Harbor

Rows of Corn

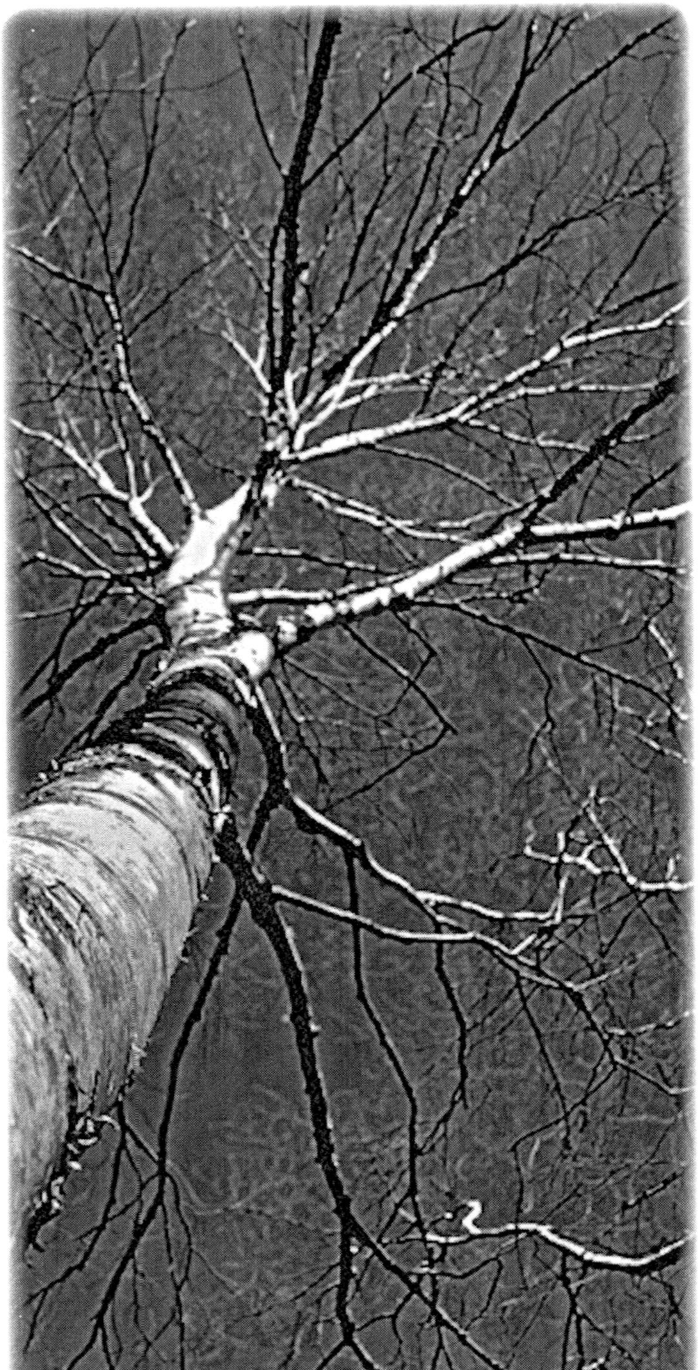

A Man and Tree

"There is history in these boughs!"
For if this is so,
        branches cannot lie,
climbing ever upward in search of the answer.

Though scarred and tattered,
The story leaves its rings.
        So does time mar with wrinkles
on each who ponder.

Neglected colors illuminate, then fade.
Through seasons of question and recurring thought,
        we seek that one swift moment,
that question in search of a tree.

Clouds

Rippled and full,
with breath,
tongues touch.

A language pure,
so fleeting
in shapes.

Listen with your eyes;
they speak,
voices soft, subtle.

The light is on.
I can see
time float,

full with life,
empty of regret
at work.

Mountains

Bits and pieces,
holding hands,
stretch and speak.

A language pure,
so nurturing
in vision.

Stories settle.
A long nap,
rock upon rock.

The light is on.
I can see
a past built.

Movement so slight,
faint whispers
at home.

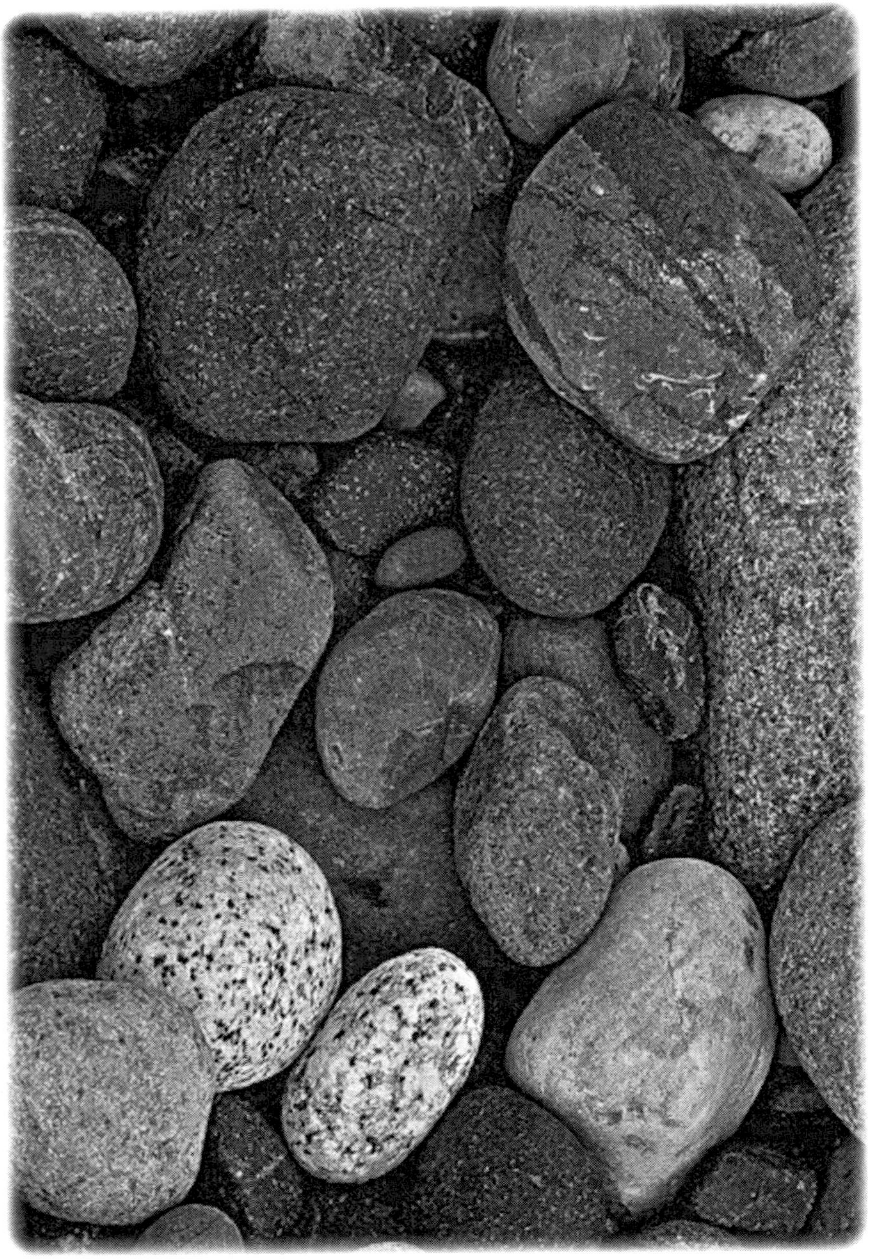

Stones

Quiet and still,
recline to reveal
an inner soul.

A language pure,
so unexpected
in colors.

Emotions vast
as the ocean,
a thousand moments.

The light is on.
I can see
faint glimmers of breath

as they lie
in each other's arms,
at rest.

Streams

Waters from above
mingle with yesterday.
Speak of tomorrow.

A language pure,
so inviting
in sound.

A moment stirs;
eyes drink in
rapt attention.

The light is on.
I can see
dreams glide by

around maypoles,
fixed in stone,
at play.

Trees

Feet so firm,
we stand,
a reverent silence.

A language pure,
so bold
in stature.

Emotion revealed
as forgotten crust
weaves time.

The light is on.
I can see
leaves dance.

I wipe my brow
and sigh, a breath shared
at peace.

Of Trees Singing

Wisp of wind and of heart,
hear us sing through leaves of thought.

Time is now and of then;
hear us sing as we bend.

Colors bloom, then sadly die;
hear us sing as seasons fly.

Bark holds fast, as leaves play fife;
hear us sing a chorus of life.

Shade to Time
Reflections from the Great Wall of China, April 8, 2001

Time slides down the slopes, caressing the seconds as it shows itself to me and to others. Stone piled onto stone compresses the time, making it compact so others may share in its secrets.

Time blooms at moments when the stone is touched. Its warmth enters the soul and provides comfort. It reveals to us the touch of others, and we reflect on that warmth and yearn to understand that time and place.

Time is revealed in shadow as that shadow clutches and pulls against the grain of stone. The heart of stone is its grain. The heart of time is that of shadow.

Time travels, stone placed upon stone. The wall stretches and grows. It seeps into the contours of the mountain it climbs. It provides protection to its builders. It provides place to those it shelters. It always will provide shade to time.

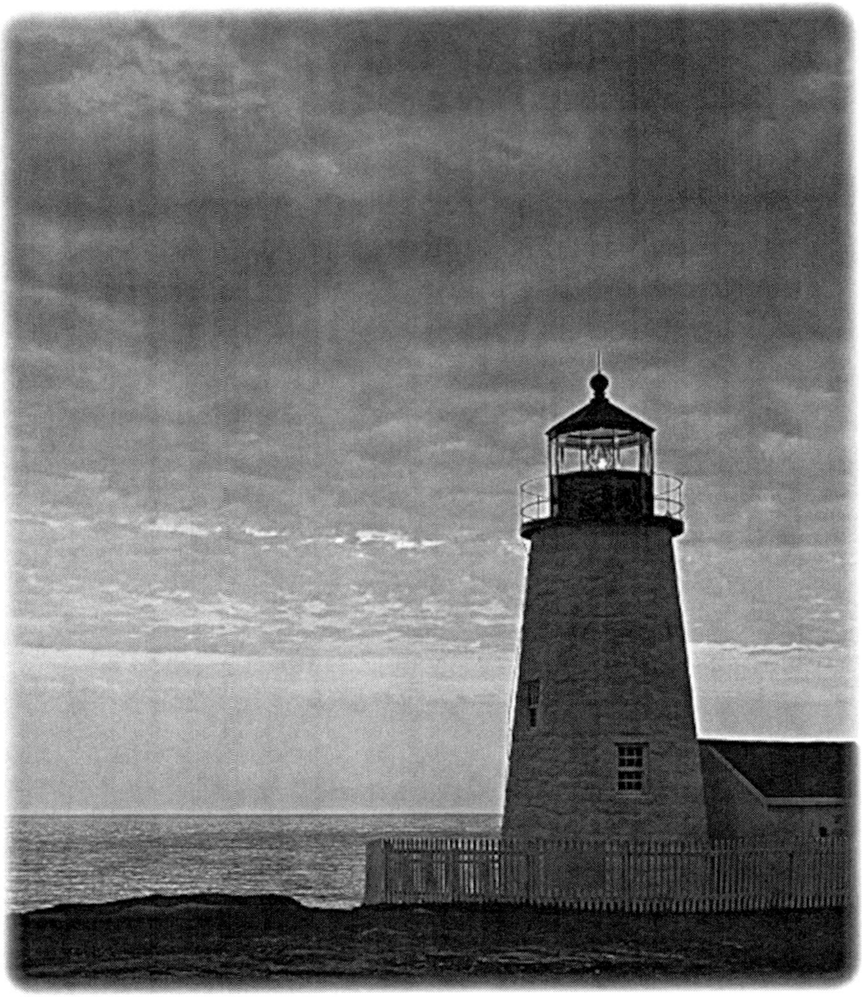

Safe Harbor
In Memory of a Friend

Such joy to make the turn.
Lonely, vacant days
try to pull me back,
but I steer her straight,
head for the sound
of land calling as seagulls wave and buoys weep.

Such joy, creased time blinks
as the rock sits,
pulling me closer,
arms outstretched in welcome.
We both exhale, make the turn,
head for the sound
of hearts melting as a mother waves and a boy weeps.

I am home.

Rows of Corn

I enter

among wide rows of mounded dirt,

kneel down,

and place within its grip

a question.

A simple seed, nourished by rain and light,

it prospers

with elements of time as friend

to grow.

I enter

among wide rows of corn

and search

for that perfect product

that upon reflection and time

will produce a smile,

and with that,

the answer I've long been

waiting for.

BOOK TWO
Some Pieces

Steps Taken

As I Wait

Night Sky

Between the Tides

Home

Beginnings

The Sound of Rain

An Endless Pause

The Touch of Another

Ebb Tide

Steps Taken
For the Soldier

Steps,
quiet and soft,
over dust,
through time.

Battle cry fades.
Clouds return.
Numb, tired
shadow.

Duty,
the call—
clouds touch,
tears fall.

Steps:
forward, strong,
hand in hand,
hold fast.

Between triumphs
rests tragedy—
moments
to remain.

Honor
the call.
Clouds touch,
tears fall.

◈

Lives suspended
within the heart.
A voice in the distance
calls from the dark.

So steps I climb;
as brothers, we climb.
Skies open; sunlight returns.
We reach; we learn.

In the aftermath,
we are because they were.
We console
and always return.

⚘

With steps taken,
a soldier dreams.
When I sleep, when I wake,
I am home,

and
so are they.

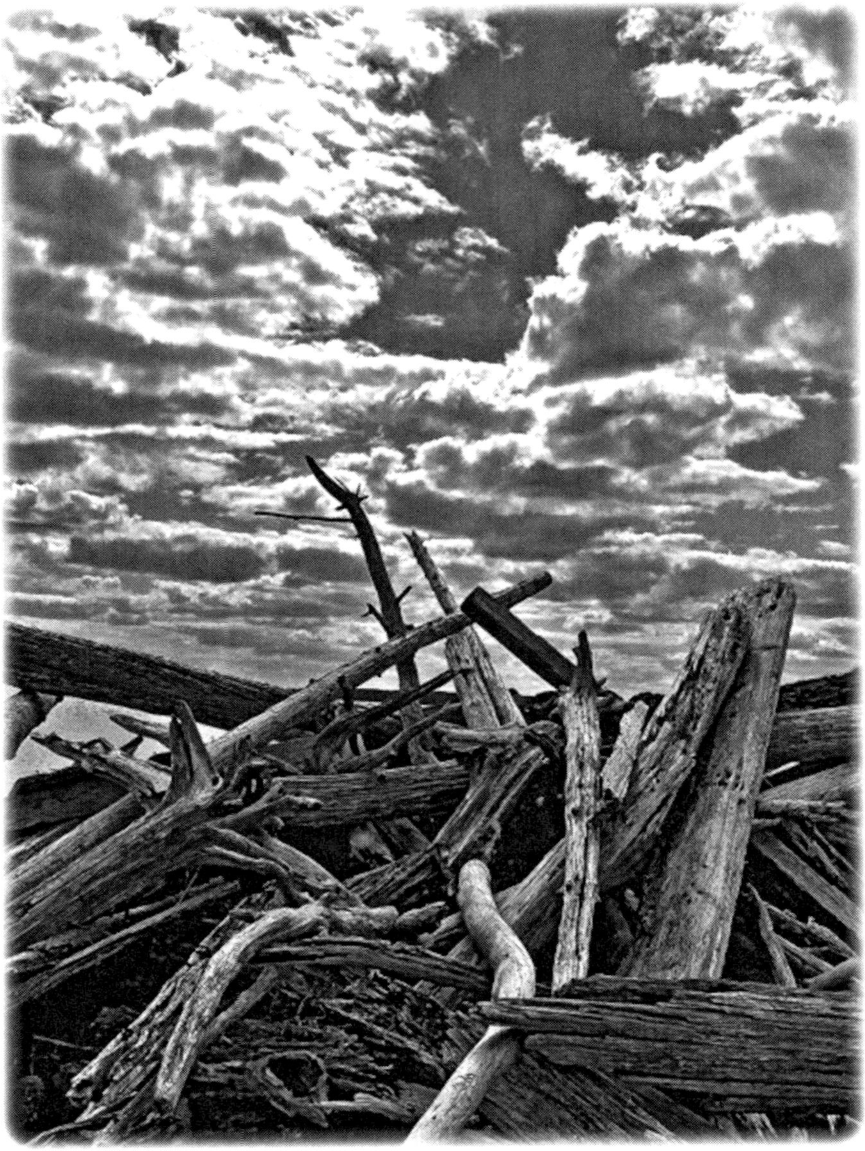

As I Wait
Reflection on September 11, 2001

There you are—a distant movement
hiding behind a corner of my mind.
I see the smile peek.

Flags, unfurled, wave in the dust.
I see colors wink from the direction
where they have been, to say "Hello."

Coming from, not going to,
a rubble so strewn, weeping
as I wait.

❦

There you are. Joy abounds,
coming around a corner to color my tears.
I touch the smile.

Flags flutter in the breeze.
I see life as we heal and clouds float
amidst the noise; white layers blink blue.

They wave as they leave
above the streets, and say "Good-bye"
as I wait.

Night Sky

We are part of everything, and because of this,
the night shines just a little bit brighter.

Looking up to the darkness, I seek something.
Unsure of what it is, I continue searching.
Glimmer of light, a color not palpable, but it
takes hold of my senses, speaks in shadows.
Cold chill, night air, stars pop with light as
salted popcorn begs a hearty laugh,
sprinkles me with its spice, as I stare in awe.

An infinite horizon is out there, beyond my gaze.
The vastness of it, the timeless wanderings of light;
where it begins is where it finally ends.
A thousand stars blink, then are gone,
only to be reborn as another again and again.
Oh, to be a star, where thoughts are placed, and
then replaced by another, so pure and magical.

Looking up to the darkness, stars glancing back,
the sky moves, waves a hello and a goodbye.
Grand in scale, I feel so small, but part
of this glorious second, minute, hour.
I move with the stars, the planets, the heavens,
and realize I am part of the magic.
Look in the mirror, at the night sky, reflected in my eyes.

Between the Tides

Life
An odyssey
to be realized,
to be lived.

Tend to the boats
and tackle.
She approaches.
Shoreline disappears.
Where has it gone?

⚜

Death
A sojourn
to be respected,
to be lived.

Take her out slow,
eyes open.
She guides.
Horizon runs forever.
Where will it go?

⚜

Time
A journey
to be realized,
to be respected.

Between the tides,
but one chance
to see
shoreline and horizon.
Where will I be?

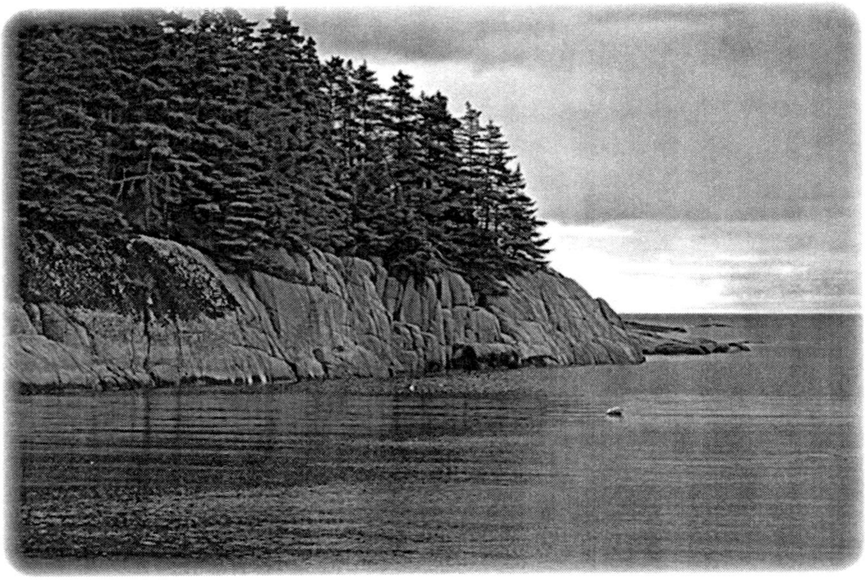

Home

I am haunted.
Ancient wood creaks; water surrounds,
cold and vacant; wind reminds memory,
her voice an echo—a faint whisper
like the clouds above, tremble, "This way, my love."

Hands worn, time given, taken, course set.
Weary oars take turns, pull upon each other.
She is with me; feel love glide atop smiles,
igniting passion lost so very long ago.

Blankets of white and gray embrace.
Stone cracked from borrowed time calls
compass-wrapped directions, to me.
We move together as one; waves breathe.

Yearning weeps; it unfurls, incomplete.
The pace quickens; heartbeat stirs to life.
Tears form unforgiving torrent, clouds part,
heaven reveals glory, creased eyes see

home.

Beginnings

Sweet refrain,
a violin speaks. The note pulsates
in twists and turns, searching for someone.
A stolen glance becomes a chance to
hear it all anew for the very
first time.
Such warmth is desire to stay and be wrapped in its embrace
while letting it find you and me, taking us to distant places.
It has happened before—so magical.

Ivory teeth,
a note sounds, the call is made.
A major effort for a minor key, seeking
solemnity revealed in pure splendor for the very
first time.
A pensive key, speaking to us of want, of desire—
perhaps to correct its bent shape, a challenge for now,
maybe forever—it continues on and on.

Canvas heavy
with intent, as colors dry a lead-laden ooze;
each stepping to the front, finding its place
as colors choose, rather than be chosen for the very
first time.
Splashes of light smile, for they are now set down as thoughts
alongside vibrant colors for us to see, to be something
stretched out on pure white—like a dream.

Nature speaks,
looking forward, never behind, as sweet raptures float,
beckon a new day in new dress while others sit, rest.
Together, we are the intrepid explorers for the very
first time.
The sun new again, we watch the sea speak lullabies as
trees dance in splendor and the wind takes all under wing
to a new place—a new beginning.

Every moment is a beginning and every
beginning a pure moment.
It is out there, perfection waiting to be found, a joyous gift of
a start and an end all wrapped together—pure harmony
just around the corner, when chance meets chance
and the end never comes;
it simply continues as a new beginning
as it is found again and again
for the very first time.

Much of my writing reflects a sense and feel of and for time. Countless thoughts of how quickly a day passes, moments, etc. My writing is an attempt to capture "it."

This piece occurred to me on a rainy morning. The window was open, and as the drops fell, the sounds peeked in under the window and dropped onto the page as words. Many times this happens in different circumstances . . . the words simply are.

&

The Sound of Rain
Reflections on Time

I am old.

With each exhale, a bit of me is lost forever.
I reach out to hold, but it slips through my grasp.

The breath, moist with memory, hangs
a bit, stops, and looks back.
It cannot return, so it gathers itself and
plunges forward, never to reappear.

Another takes its place, but it too looks
back, remembers, and is gone.
With each inhale, I try to call back time: a
memory, a past moment, a piece of me.

We breathe to live; we breathe to remember.

Rain . . . long lost memories, thoughts from us all fall, touching us with moist embraces of the past. Its smell is of childhood . . . of ball games and hopscotch, of bubble gum and bikes, tattered jeans and worn-out sneakers, friendship.

I love the sound of rain.

An Endless Pause

*Skip a stone and it will eventually sink to the bottom,
but the ripples it creates, go on and on . . . Forever*

༄

A house stands neglected and alone by the edge of a
pond. Sitting and waiting while time moves around
it in fractal seconds, becoming long, quick years
that simply sneak up when no one is looking.

The years moved by fast,
so flattered to be, but still to prove.
A stone is gripped by my hand.
Its smoothness
reminds of time gone by, its edge, of distant possibilities.

Thrown in haste, with delight,
it looks back with regret, tries
to stay while moving forward.
Its smoothness
remains on my fingers as its toes skip across the surface.

Then with a last breath, it sinks to the bottom.

The ripples stretch and roll, awaken
for the first time, as wakes form
and roll with precision,
their smoothness
in slow motion, look back as they curl with memory.

And,

in the midst of a bird's wings, the ocean's waves,
a child's giggle and a mother's joy, a mountain's rapture,
a breath . . . running water, a distant call, a rustle of leaves,
tears shed, surprise revealed . . . the
minutes, the hours, the days.

A flicker of light reveals peeling paint.

There is a pause . . . if captured, it is endless.

The Touch of Another

We are here for such a brief time, yet the footprints made are cherished by others, long after we are gone.

Loving embrace,
mother to child,
never pales
when light
fades
to darkness;
nurtured,
it grows
always.

Fingers laced,
father to son,
contact made
this day, every day,
seen
and unseen,
firm
with wisdom
always.

Eyes meet a
friend of mine,
voice intent,
listening
to all
that is said,
and hearing
all that is not
always.

A piano key is touched ever so lightly. A note is born and travels, like the ripples of a pebble thrown from shore, or a breath smiling on the pane as it slides . . . a note tucked into a book, or footprints in the sand . . . when lost, we find

The touch of another
is there
to remind,
bringing peace,
certain comfort,
and tears,
serene sincerity
and a smile
always.

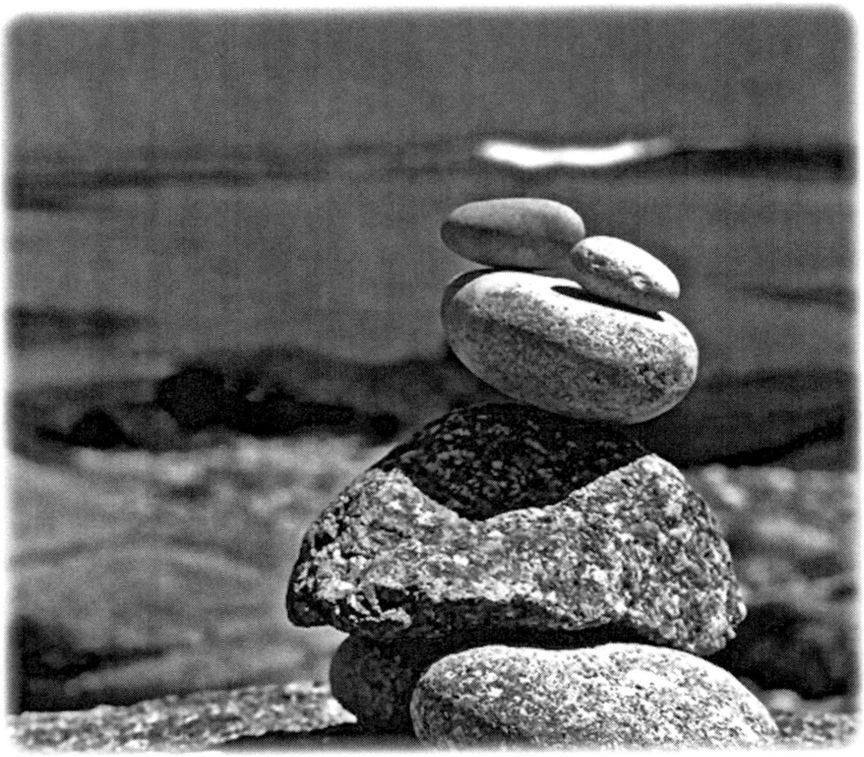

Ebb Tide

I stand on the shore, one with the sand,

looking at today, searching for tomorrow.
Light is everywhere, separated by horizon:
blue above, blue green below;
white patches cling to both.

     ❦

Watching as the air takes each breath away,
and salt takes its place in my soul.
Water flows away from the shore
not high or low, but away . . .

Gulls fly high, looking back to remember.
Their feathers caress the air so lightly,
move like the water, coming and going,
life's presence fulfilled by air and sea.

I smile as waves fall, rolling effortlessly.
Coming back, returning as if by chance,
the place where it all started, home.
The sea knows its return is endless.

⁂

I stand on the shore, one with the sand,

looking at today, finding tomorrow.
The ebb tide recedes with my thoughts and hopes
flowing away with the gulls' laughter,
leaving, in its place, peace.

BOOK THREE
And Story

An Evening of Grace

As Water Beckons

A Journey

Touching of Souls

Possession Morning

Holding Grace

Washed Anew

Beyond Beautiful

A Morning Made of Perfection

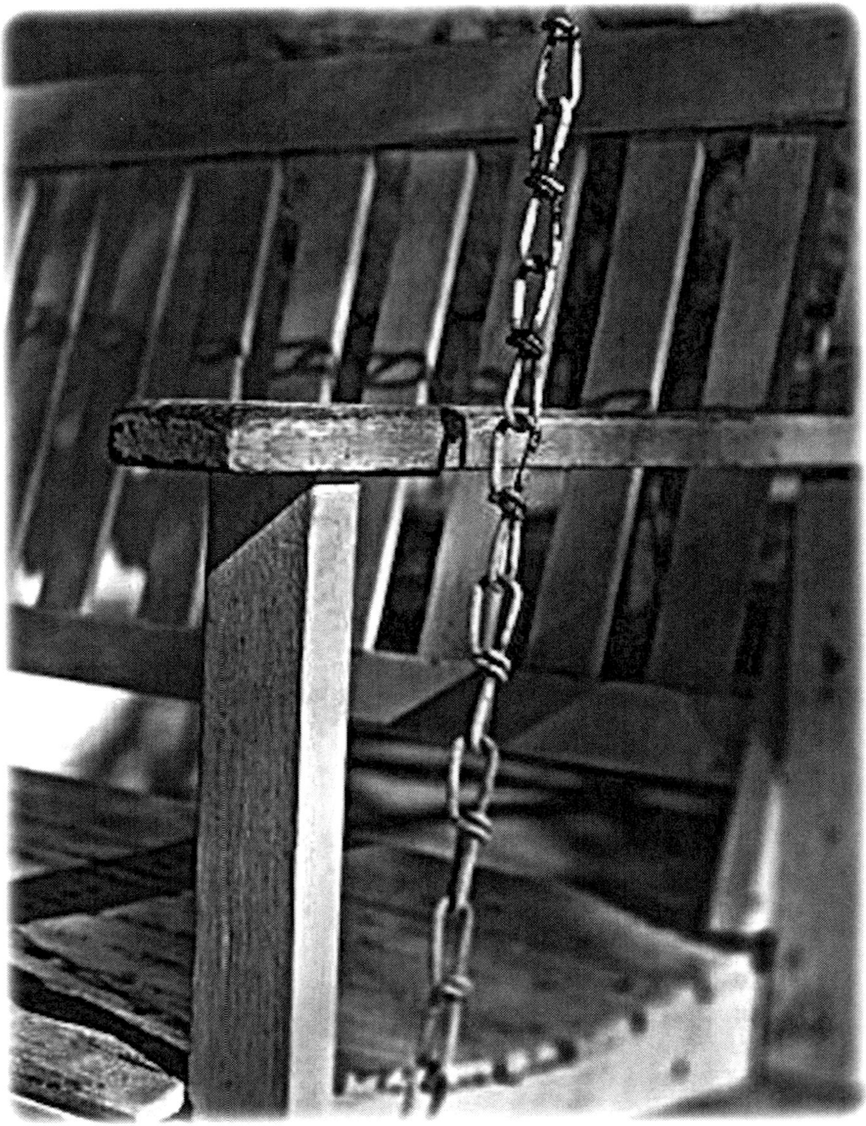

An Evening of Grace

The trees watch as the evening light recedes, reflecting on a day full of life—of possibilities found and those missed. So do I, as I sit. The porch swing glides forward and back in a magical, dreamlike rhythm. Like being in a mother's arms, wrapped and warmed with blankets and breath, a cadence that soothes the soul.

Life is surreal sometimes if we pause and take a moment . . .

> a glance made to the yard in front, the street just beyond. The one from my childhood, days filled with laughter and scraped knees. A street open with possibility and void of flaws. The air, crisp with memory, flaunts itself every now and then. It starts to rain. How magic is the sound of rain?

The trees blink with the last of the light, trying to hold on to the day. I strain to see with squinted eyes, as creases and wrinkles scratch and claw to surface, and take part in the memory of a tree and a boy . . .

> in younger days, the climb would be quick—up, up through the branches, feel the rough edges of bark, regret . . . and the subtle softness of the new wood and buds, possibility . . . all the while gazing out on days past, through the leaves, touch it, feel it.

The days and years reach out and embrace me again. I can see them, oh, so clearly. The rain, it falls in sequence, a pattern, so light it seduces.

As I am, the sound of the chain speaks to me, link by link, metal against metal, bits and pieces flake, and fragments fall to the ground or separate and take flight to another place. Some wait for tomorrow and call me back to this moment today.

The trees have closed their eyes, at least for now. It is dark, yet still so bright. The heavens above speak in tones of morning dew, of a day still to come. Branches let go. I return to the earth and realize no more, my time now grounded. On this porch swing, gentle movement is all I can muster as the chains stretch and defy gravity. They support; they speak in caked tones of yesterday, rusted proof of time.

Now still and quiet, the porch swing moves within me, gliding back and forth in memory, like a clock, a pendulum of life. I inhale and exhale in syncopation as rain falls. Gracious for the time spent, it now washes everything—over everything, through everything, even me. Evening lies down and night wakes up. Sounds from the street float with an echo, embrace the rain with rapture, for it is memory of a day, a time that keeps pace when we no longer can. A full chorus, harmony for all, back and forth, kept in rhythm by the heart.

I can hear it so clearly.

As Water Beckons

Listen quietly; be still.
A magical refrain is played,
the sweetness of its notes embrace, become one.
A song, perhaps a child of oboe, piano,
thoughts of two nurtured by water.

It surrounds; it comforts
with breath and laugh, saddened regret
balanced by lingering moments, lost
so very long ago, yet so close . . . caked with salt,
it reminds, just as ripples seek their place.

A drop with purpose, takes notice . . .

forms on a leaf, hangs forever
frozen, contemplates. It is, therefore, we are.
The drop falls with delight,
remembering as it goes, yesterday, today, and
tomorrow too, so bright and oh, so blue.

Swirling drops dance together,
brush by with giggles sweet and pure,
fall to the ground, as memories
sponged by time, caressed with love,
collect in pools cool and clear, waiting.

Beauty wrapped in water, determined . . .

with constancy, urging regret, moves on,
gurgling for air, rolling with life.
It always seeks a path, a wayfarer
clouded by time, nourished by sun.
It calms, it speaks, forever.

As docile streams seek benevolent rivers
water begets oceans, calm seas
for you and for me.
Collective thoughts for sure, a light
revealed, standing with closed eyes.

The sound, like that of a loving voice . . .

with shell to ear, listen, feel
a warm touch that whispers with love,
and memories which calm the discourse,
the fumbling rhetoric of life,
and fills it with ...

gulls dancing upon the wind, happy to simply be.
Caps swirling with envy, vying for place,
slapping with frolic in foam delight, as
tides speak in sweet rapture of time and place.
The water echoes as she speaks; he listens
to all that is and is not said.
Winds from afar, ignited by passion so long ago, shout
with laughter and pure solitude as the voices of family,
friends, and faces past and present speak within the
waves, rolling with purpose as eternal companions.

We are never alone, when with the sea.

As water beckons,
I sip what remains
of you, perhaps of me,
always together, with hands and hearts
guided by the waves.

A Journey
January 31, 2010

We experience because to do so means we are alive. We experience life through our interactions with people and places. Not because they are there, but because a small piece of who we are, is.
We are in all places.

From the day we are born, a small fragment of who we are, or more importantly, who we will become, is waiting to be found. Waiting to be realized and, at the same time, become a part of our life. The life and the path we choose to follow.

From all corners of the world, in the mountains, the seas, the jungles, the deserts, the vast arctic landscape, the canyons, the coastlines, and within the clouds of time, they wait. The journey we all make is a journey to be found, to be complete.

My journey is about experiencing these places and people, and in so doing, reclaiming a piece of me, a lost fragment waiting to be discovered. Making me more complete now, this moment, than before.

Steps, and there will be many of them, one at a time, taking me that much closer to the end of the journey where I am not yet complete, but happy, and look back with a smile, to a life well lived.

The Arctic waits . . .

Touching of Souls
Reflections on Life

The clouds move and have rhythm to their shape. They change as my eyes fall upon them. They are constant with motion, restless to a fault. They move and breathe, as do I. I look upon them, and they upon me.

Life seeks shape while being different.

A storm approaches, and I take shelter. Close to windows so I may see the tempest approach. Protected from the fury, I am still part of it. I travel inside it, and it carries me to another place where I can be me, simply me.

Life seeks others while being solitary.

The wind provides shape to the light and color, proof of existence. I press close to the window. With each breath, a little of me is left on the pane. Light reflects through that pane, the breath takes flight. I watch as it leaves, like a bird on the wing, gliding between clouds. Always searching.

Life seeks purpose while being reflective.

Raindrops run down the pane, not falling, but stretching to remain. I recall a childhood of laughter, joy, and sadness. Rain always ended a day of play. Now, older, we remember our younger days when it rains. Seeing and hearing the drops fall takes us back to that time.

Life seeks happiness while being collective.

The rain has stopped, clouds part and sunlight splashes against my face. I take in the warmth, and know that others do the same. Perhaps a stranger, a friend, or even a lost love feels the sun's warmth. How good it is to feel the sun, and know others near and far do the same. A pure, shared moment.

Life is a journey of the soul and that journey has no end.

A breath long ago took flight, reaching up to touch the clouds. I long for that breath, but understand, it does not die. It rests beside the others, waiting for the precise moment when the clouds will gather, nurture each other, remember days, and, at last, touch and become one.

Possession Morning

Fragments of a dream simmer, like cream rising to the top of coffee, only to be pushed down by the swirling motion of the spoon in my fingers. Pushed down by me while trying to keep distance between now and the morning.

The aroma wafts up and pries at the heaviness of a day trying to arrive. The thoughts of the night meander and coalesce above me like talons of some ancient raptor diving into my flesh, seeking the vein that contains all. They are distant, yet so close, as dreams sometimes are. At times, they come together. It is like that, you know.

The fragrance melds with the light. A light not omnipresent, but sometimes present, like dreams. Giving a nudge and sometimes a wink. Simply being there. A smack of cold water on the face runs down the fabric of aroma and light. It is different each and every morning, as I lull in my chair, trying to push back and contain the moment.

It escapes, as always, a shrouded beggar looking and seeking more. The street outside, with its jumbled mass of humanity waiting. I can hear it. I sip the hot liquid, and as it slides down, I am warmed on the inside as sunlight seeps through the curtain onto my face and warms me on the outside. The footfalls outside strike pavement, pushing the light and my dreams with them.

This morning, I am up and now ready for the day. The dreams that once were will be again. I will return, and they will go on. All the while in my mind, I think and calculate a cunning way to capture them, and place distance between the morning and my dreams. In the end, as I step onto the pavement, deep down I know I will never possess them, for they already possess me.

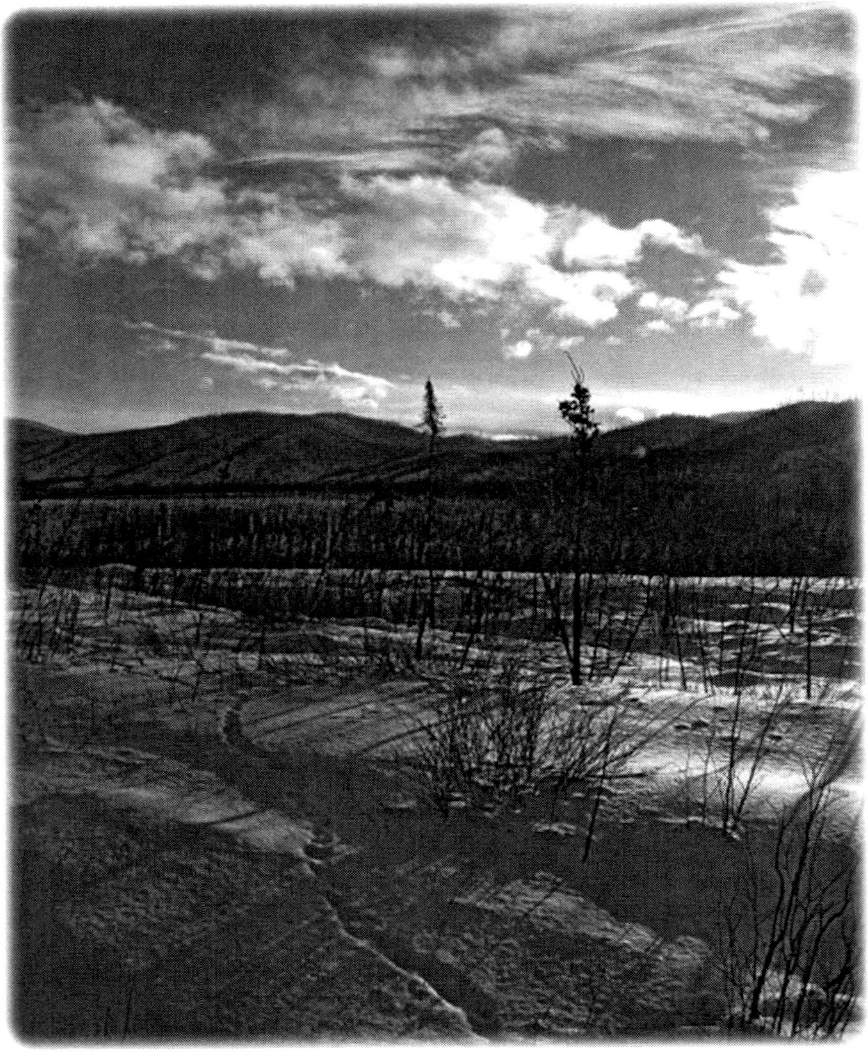

Holding Grace

Cupping my hands, I blow into them an assortment of memories. For an instant, the heat is felt and a smile rises. But the relentless cold seeps in, takes hold, and sprinkles them lightly with today. The memories stretch and yawn, come alive within my grip, like tiny dancers in a globe swirling with chaos, yet subtle with precision as they float, then fall.

There they lightly sit, suspended on a layer of pure white snow. Fragmented crystals of captured light and memory lying in wait. Time displayed on a magical carpet of wonder and beauty that taunts with its cold and warms the heart with silence. I am here and so are they. With quiet as companion, I walk with every sense vulnerable, open, and waiting to receive . . . my eyes listen.

The morning light, with fingers stretched, reaches for the edge that is not there. Knowing this and a little of that, it pursues its prey while paying little interest to those distant and not so very far away. It approaches and engulfs the senses as pupils constrict and focus, closing out the light in order to see. Really see. I stand transfixed.

The crust on which I stand speaks with every crack and echoes through the trees of place and beauty. The snow, as it falls, brushes past pine needles and bark, grabbing their essence and moving on, to lie on the ground dormant, waiting.

The sun touches and warms as the day moves on, revealing bits and pieces of hidden movement within the corners. A burden shared with the animals as they, too, seek their veiled turn on the magical carpet, leaving momentary traces of themselves, to be found, perhaps, only once. How those footprints speak to me. An experience shared by two. Somewhere a rabbit breathes —I do too, here.

The stream, as it meanders over the slumber of fallen trees and stones, seeks a path . . . sometimes new, many times old, so it can return to where it all began. It drifts and rolls while singing with siren's voice to those in range. The sound is a lullaby to my ears as it sings of those who came before, and now calls all life to its banks, to drink from its cup.

The starlings up high in the drafts murmur their time through the clouds. Every now and then, one appears out of line, then corrects. A cloud of birds all traveling together, they circle and dive in a spectacle that brings a smile. A gull gets too close, is quickly scolded, and moves on. A symphony of movement, and I am here watching and hoping it lasts forever.

The trees are now in front of me, just at the edge of the clearing. In the corner sits a cluster of birches with their white teeth gleaming in the light, a grin so big within the dense green, it blinds. I stand firm to look and take in their beauty. They are an exclamation point rising out of the crusted snow in an attempt to show direction, or simply a nice place to sit and revel in the day.

As I turn to leave this place, the far off sound of a woodpecker leaving his mark can be heard. Perhaps a future home or a respite for weary travelers. The tree, no doubt, is accommodating his needs quite well with a subtle handshake. I soon find my steps keeping time with his punctuation of the tree. Funny how things seem to simply find each other and come together in a rhythm all their own.

How the hours have passed. The crunch made with each and every footfall is a call back to that chasm of pure silence. The essence of life all around me points with direction, like breadcrumbs seeking paths through reticent thoughts. Pure thoughts all as one, comrades in arms through thick and thin, quiet desperation wrapped in exhilaration. I walk and return home after a day well spent.

In a tired time, with the light outside drifting away for another day and the lights inside flickering as they come to life, I cup my hands together and prepare to give thanks . . . to the life of a day given to me. A day shared with past and present, living and dying, of body and not, and a realization that in everything that is, there is something that was.

As I think of this, the day reclines. The light seeps from the folds of the field and stream, brushes past as the starlings head home, lands lightly on the nose of a rabbit, and waves a good-bye to the woodpecker nestled in his home. The day is done, at least for now. But it will awake with the light's return and open its arms again, holding me with everything I see and touch, in everything I share with this life, together wrapped in grace.

Washed Anew

He has been gone a long time.

The man walks, steps taken, always looking down
never forward, a stare in search of something.
Air heavy with moisture, with life,
trees dappled by light make shadow.
All around, the sweat is heavy and deliberate.

The rails ignore as sunlight winks with direction.
Stones ricochet off metal, sing a morning air.
Steps taken with time, one after the other.
The sound of stones keep company, a cadence
as rhythm sings and time meets dull metal.

Shoes marked by life, clothes heavy with purpose,
gravity pulls, unbuttoned and exposed.
Thin strands of thread hold on, long days,
blind rails rusted with neglect, tired years.
He walks as the tracks stretch, rail by rail.

Tired thoughts give way as a sigh is made.
Letters escape, float and swirl in puffs of dust,
crop circles form high above, a distant haze.
Letters mingle, chatter, finally form and rest as words,
collected yet loose, poetic potential.

Dust-caked words taunt; they travel, but cling,
vagabonds on clothes, on life. Never truly friend,
they are distant, and so is he.
He gives of himself, but no one is there,
exhales a tired breath, and tries to remember.

Perhaps words from the past, times as a young boy,
as the rails reach, metal lies dormant and forgotten,
rust piled up, a life of childhoods over and over again;
both lives a congealed mass of words misplaced, orphans
neglected as lost time collects and builds, layer upon layer.

From behind, his train approaches.

The whistle bellows and wakes all around. Leaves of trees fold, flowers turn, as stones shake and roll. A daydream ends as the train approaches. He is startled as the tiniest of hairs align and shriek in annoyance. The rails begin to speak as bits and pieces of red jump and alight into the air as confetti, shouting, "Wake up, wake up." He continues to walk with the air around him hanging silently in anticipation, longing and hoping for that push. The train's speed is deceiving as cars blink in shadows like postcards passing by, backwards they wave with regret, while the air, once calm, is frenzied and pushes the fugitive words by him. The train races by and then evaporates, but the breeze from it lingers as it tries to pull everything with it. Take it down the rails, on its own journey. With eyes closed and the air boiling all around, distant memories tug and pull voices and images to the surface with recollection and surprise. He opens his eyes and smiles as he gazes down the track, seeing younger days, his tattered clothes hanging by the slimmest of threads, and the hat waving good-bye . . .

With fresh green all around, a boy pants with excitement, trying to see what lies around the bend. Trees scratch and claw, holding him back, but relentless pursuit wins out. Air crisp with blue jeans and bubble gum, the boys ahead are winning as path yields paths, some clear slopes for speed and few gullies for rest. In view, the rope lies dormant and lonely. Worn from years of use, with sweat and laughter resting in wait. Waiting to reveal the stories held within its strands. Just through the trees, deep blue glistens in the afternoon's fading light as wisps of white reflect up from the surface, a snapshot of what circles overhead. Forgetting the others, the boy bounds from rock to rock, close to the edge, then leaps with a determined reach, grabs hold and continues through the trees to deep, dark blue waters. With white halo as accent, the cherub flies with outstretched arms and for a few brief seconds, hangs in the silent air as he thinks of . . .

Days of clean clothes and endless sunshine embraced as one in a never-ending sky of blue. One that wrapped tight, squeezing laughs and surprise to the surface. Vibrant smells and colors so fresh like an apple pie oozing with sweetness, of cherry blossoms unfolding themselves up toward the light, a shimmering light, forever free. Friends and family hidden in time, returning from shadows to remind, as they quietly nudge more of themselves and his memories to the surface.

He begins to step quietly and deliberate, with a new sense of the day and an unfamiliar purpose. A trove of returning memories, realized at this very moment, as he smiles and listens . . . to the rails glistening in the sunlight speak of men toiling with perspiration and song, as they heave the heavy load together, laying down timber and steel with song and story, surprising him with emotion, providing comfort and a push to explore all at the same time, within himself and beyond, to reach out, to touch and hold possible stories within a story, his story. He moves on.

Looking back from where we are . . .

We see rails smooth and fresh, glowing with sunlight,
polished perfection, they now speak
as the slough of old is set free to mingle
with the letters, the words laden with experience,
and journey to find their place, to find him.

We see acceptance of a day, this day,
a time, his time, a chance to begin again,
steps taken fresh and new, as in the beginning,
as a child clinging to that rope, a rope of days
flying with a breeze in his face, muscles tense.

We see the boy fly, dusted cares wiped clean,
a man letting go for an eternity, forever,
the cool water reaching into his soul,
a soul now revealed in tears and joy.
The hat returns; he picks it up and continues.

He had been gone a long time.

Long strides now replace forgotten ones,
moving, no longer solitary but full of promise,
remembering friends and experience as mentors,
eyes moving side to side, taking it all in,
a day bright with breath, dripping with possibility.

Memory gives life and purpose to him, the reward.
It is on everything; it is in everything,
waiting to fly, looking forward to tomorrow,
washed anew with baptismal grace,
the man and his life now one.

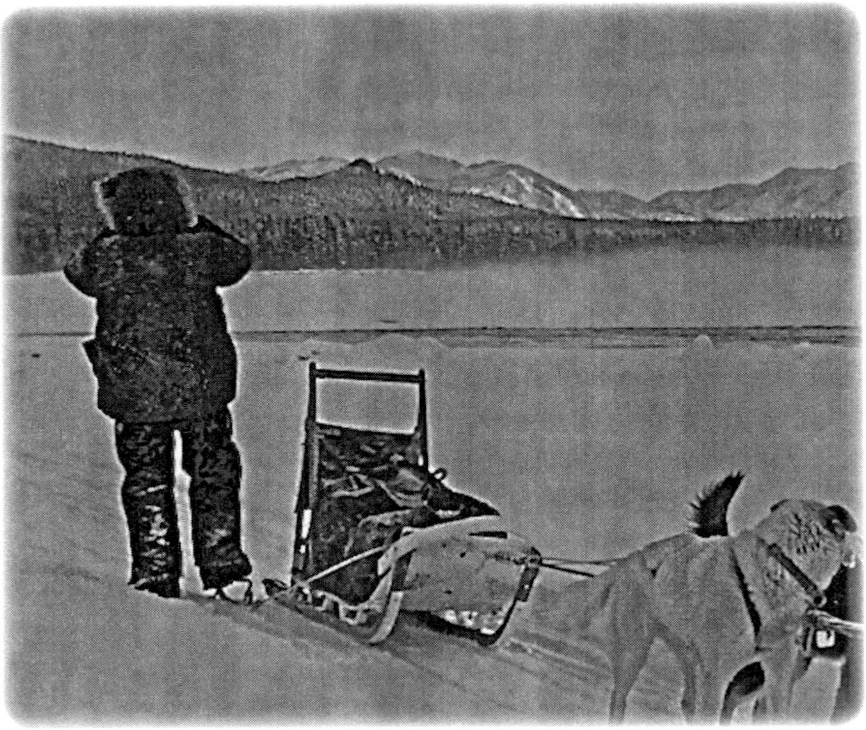

Beyond Beautiful
Dog Sledding the Yukon Territory, Alaska

A ghost lingers at the edge of the world,
trying to touch, to feel, to be alive.
White chill air blows in from the north.
Icy arms reach from nowhere; they grasp firm,
take me to this periphery, the world
and the life of my soul.

Frigid cold screams, "Look at me!"
wants to live, become me, survive this moment.
Pallid glimpses of grainy color seep
everywhere. I breathe them in and hold,
question the beauty that lies underneath,
buried perfection waiting to bloom.

Through clenched eyes I see ...

Tall naked pines climbing to touch the sky, towering above, they seek their own answers as green specs blink through white and yearn for yesterday. Tomorrow is too far to see as the cold returns to remind me that I am here, and so is it. Again the cold pounds with its touch and breath, so brutally cold it warms my soul. I feel alive for the first time, but in my head I know it cannot be true. I stand, remembering many moments and looking out to the distant landscape as it envelops me, and I try to catch this one. Tuck it away for another day, while within my heart, pure joy and exhilaration exclaim with each beat, "I am here."

Majestic rocks yearn for warmth as they guide, absorb the cold as white turns grey. The shadows creep from corners, eager to return to take their place. Fatherly, they stand at attention and wave me on as I pass by. A rush of the breeze and cold caress the stone as it brushes by my face, with smells of fresh old thoughts and of dogs. The panting of now bounces off the walls to collect and mingle with the sound of this place to reveal a canyon's voice. The passage sounds of dogs and sled combine with the voice, adding strength, direction. So many sounds collide and come together as I try to speak with fragile words. In this place, I can only speak softly the words; listen, forever, the echo ...

Perpetual snow is spotted and speckled with life. Tracks come and go as they crisscross one life over the other in a maze of fur, skin, and bone. The dogs tender the trail and push on in the cold, hearts beating together as a cadence is born. The sled glides and follows in stubborn pursuit out of canyons high to sheer glaze of winter's tongue of ice and water. The river breathes underneath and moves as we travel above, wondering if we will ever meet. Heart beats fast as we push, then push again, over this frozen bridge of escape and joy, to paths beyond its grip. We stand, fixed in this moment, fixed in time. Together we look at two paths but need only one, and find it has chosen us.

Itinerant sunlight making its presence known with feeble attempts to show me the way. It speaks amidst the shadows and life that is seen and unseen. Its light reaches into the nuances of the day and brings life to the very simplest of things. The colors smile back with each and every touch, revealing the souls that lie asleep among the pines, rocks, and river solid. With all that has occurred, and will again for others who follow my lead, follow my path, the magical moments await, as the shades are drawn for yet another day. I stand in this moment, with sadness and a numbing reminder of the cold, as the shadows slowly tread their way toward me as I remember to weep not for shadows, as they are reminders of the day.

Frigid cold stares as I scream back, "Look at me!"
having lived, become this place, survived this moment,
vibrant glimpses of smooth colors pour forth
everywhere. I breathe them in and hold,
accept the beauty once buried, now
revealed, perfection in full bloom, within.

A ghost revealed to me, the journey,
a lost fragment within me, now found
to be experienced again and again.
A memory of this place and time,
of cold and white, of color and life,
beyond beautiful.

A Morning Made of Perfection

The cold air resides at the door. *Outside.*

Knocking for acceptance, it yearns to share in the warmth and glad tidings waiting on the other side. *Inside.*

The windowpane, all frost bound and smoldering both inside and out, blinks pure white. Snow-laden trees dance with every push of the wind. *Silence.*

The room sits undisturbed and pale except for the red-orange embers of the fire flickering in the early morning light. Remembering last night's hurried pace, they slumber, yet still offer a hearty welcome. *Warmth.*

The air, thick with the scent of pine, drapes itself over everything, while last night's hot chocolate tingles the nose of every child still dreaming of what awaits. *Magic.*

Colored lights flicker with the slightest movement, while white lights sit erect and steadfast on the windowsill, showing the way to would-be travelers seeking respite from the cold night air. *Welcome.*

The floorboards creak as steps are made from upstairs to down. Small puffs of fragrant, smoky dust trail far behind and show direction to the eye of a child that lies awake. *Waiting.*

Happy packages lie in silver and red wrappings. Bows grin like the Cheshire Cat waiting to be plucked, pulled, and tossed in a forgotten heap. The gift concealed inside lovingly placed, not so long ago, by hands careful to preserve the thought and love hidden within, soon to be opened and shared. *Revealed.*

The outside light is brighter as it chases away the cold and says, "Hello" to the crystals of snow on the pane, the flickering lights on the tree, the wrapped packages sitting beneath evergreens, the warm, soft glow of the fire, the bounty of ornaments, the eyes of the family gathered, and the glistening of life's breath as it joins together in this special and magical morning. *Love.*

On a morning made of perfection, a family gathers and love is revealed. Love of the day, a moment, eternal. It is a morning more special than those before and others soon to follow. It is a morning filled with family, friends, and faith. It is one of hope, love and joy. It is a morning made for you, for me, for everyone. *Perfection.*

Notes